I CHOOSE TO Live!

Arletha Orr

Kingdom Trailblazers Publishing

To the one who feels alone, you're not.

Hey hey!

I've struggled with this for months. I initially wanted to do a devotion, but I have too much to say to limit it. I wanted to speak directly from the heart and lead you all through the steps or things I felt while going through grief. I guess we can call it my diary!

If you do not know my story, please purchase my book titled Live! It will help you understand that things are penned in this diary.

In this diary, you will see the good, bad, and the ugly. I'm being transparent to let you know that we all go through these things, but you are not alone.

It hurts! It's a shame the way some act, but it's cool. God is still God and will help you through it all.

I love you all and I pray this gives you the strength to keep going.

Love you!

DAY 1

"It's okay to not be okay"

It's a common thing for someone to ask, "how are you?" and we reply, "I'm okay!" Knowing deep down inside I want to fall out on the floor, kick and scream to the top of my lungs because I am in disbelief about what just happened to me!

Why am I here? How did I get here? We'll get to that later. If you're not okay, express that to whomever or express it to God. I remember telling God that I am not okay, and I need Your help to get through this. Be honest with yourself. It's necessary for healing.

You too can go to God and say, "God, I'm not okay. I'm feeling angry today and I need strength to make it through the day!" Because He is God, guess what He will do, He's going to see about His child and honor your request. Grief is not an easy process. It is natural and okay to experience those different emotions and feelings. The amazing part is you don't have to feel it alone. The scripture says that the Holy Spirit is our Comforter. He will help you through it all. Just believe and trust in Him.

Scripture: But the Helper, the Holy Spirit, whom the Father will send in My name, He will teach you all things, and bring to your remembrance all things that I said to you. John 14:26 NKJV

Question: What can I release and give to God?

_____

_____

_____

_____

_____

_____

_____

_____

_____

_____

_____

_____

_____

_____

_____

_____

_____

DAY 2

"The Struggle to Believe"

Has anybody ever just been stuck where they are and couldn't believe their reality? If you hadn't, I have. It took me months and I can probably say at least two years to finally accept the fact that my family was no longer with me. I would often have moments where I would say "man I can't believe they're gone!" Most people will be missing a person, but I had to miss 3 whole humans, at once.

Often when we're going through, it's hard to trust God when we can't trace Him. It's hard to trust God to help me be happy when I just lost my husband. It's hard to trust God when I just lost my two children, but people say, "it will be alright." It's hard to trust God when I just lost my best friend. It's hard to trust God to go to this job every day but the people are constantly getting on my nerve. It's hard to trust God when I'm going through trials and tribulations in my life!

The Bible states that faith is the substance of things hoped for and the evidence of things not seen. So, it's safe to say even when we can't feel God or even when we can't see God moving, our faith says that He's already worked it out. Even though I don't have money in my bank account, my faith says my family is already fed. Even though the doctors gave me a bad report, my faith says I'm healed! Even though I just lost my world, God says He will mend my broken heart. Activate your faith and trust God!

Scripture: Now faith is the substance of things hoped for, the evidence of things not seen. Hebrews 11:1 NKJV

Question: Do you have faith?

_____

_____

_____

_____

_____

_____

_____

_____

_____

_____

_____

_____

_____

_____

_____

_____

_____

DAY 3

Giving up is not an option!

Have you ever wanted to give up? Have you ever felt as if this is not the life you're supposed to have and you're just willing to let it all go? Me!! I've been there.

After my family returned to the Creator, there was this moment when I wanted my life to end. I had no reason to live right!? My ONLY husband and my ONLY children were gone. What was my purpose? Why did I have to stay? Why didn't God take me?

I was driving one day, and I said God, you can just take me too. I have no reason to live. They were all I had. Work, church, and family! That was me! That was us! But I was playing with my cell phone while driving and almost ran off the road. Immediately, I could hear my baby say "Mama it's not your time. You have a purpose!"

I begin to cry like a baby. I mean real ugly tears. I wanted to leave but apparently, it wasn't part of His plan.

God did not bring you this far to leave you. He has equipped you for what you're going through. The cliché' is "He gives the toughest battles to His strongest soldiers!" When we feel like it gets too hard to bear, God is our comfort and guide to give us strength and hope to keep going. Don't give up! You're almost to the finish line!

Scripture: …the race is not to the swift, nor the battle to the strong, nor bread to the wise, nor riches to men of understanding, nor yet favour to men of skill; but time and chance happeneth to them all. Ecclesiastes 9:11 NKJV

Question: What promises do you have to stand on?

_____

_____

_____

_____

_____

_____

_____

_____

_____

_____

_____

_____

_____

_____

_____

_____

_____

DAY 4

"What is the plan for my life?"

Most people don't know, well I guess that the whole world will know now. But on the day of the accident, I was supposed to pick my babies up from school. My husband worked at night so sometimes he would sleep, and we would take turns picking them up in the afternoon.

My husband called me thirty minutes before I was scheduled to leave work that day and said that he would pick them up from school. I was never on time for work, so I needed a few more minutes on the clock, so I decided to stay later than my normal time.

Well, on my way home is when I received the call. So why didn't God allow me to pick them up that day? What does God have planned for my life? I'm here for a reason. God said it and my baby said it.

What is God's plan for your life? You've been through it all, but you're still here. Things you thought you wouldn't survive, you did. When you thought, you weren't going to make it, you did! Will you still accomplish what He has for you?

Scripture: For I know the thoughts that I think toward you, says the Lord, thoughts of peace and not of evil, to give you a future and a hope. Jeremiah 29:11 NKJV

Question: What is my purpose?

_____

_____

_____

_____

_____

_____

_____

_____

_____

_____

_____

_____

_____

_____

_____

_____

DAY 5

"Where is God?"

Where is God? We know He's always there, but it doesn't feel like it. When He called my family back to Him, there was a time I thought, "how did He allow this to happen?" Whew! I was heartbroken! But I had to realize that God is sovereign.

They teach us these things in the church and trust me, I needed everything I was taught! I need all the Bible knowledge and Word because this is hard. But isn't that what it's for? It's for us to remind Him so that He can help us when we're going through it.

Often when we're going through it, we think God has left us. We cry, pray, cry, and pray more…and it seems like God is nowhere nearby. The Bible says when the poor man cried out, God heard him and saved him from his troubles. Don't get discouraged when you cry out and feel like God isn't hearing you, because guess what, He does! And He's there to tend to your every need.

Scripture: This poor man cried out, and the Lord heard him, and saved him out of all his troubles. Psalms 34:6 NKJV

Question: Where do you need God in your life?

_____

_____

_____

_____

_____

_____

_____

_____

_____

_____

_____

_____

_____

_____

_____

_____

_____

DAY 6

Loneliness

If you have children, you will understand the noise level in a house. Because you're a mom and you have dealt with it for so long, it becomes your norm, right?! Children will be children. You can't make them be quiet and act like statues forever.

There was NEVER a quiet moment in our house. Well, except for when everyone was asleep but other than that, we were all the way live. I had a husband, a seven-year-old daughter, and a one-year-old son. Thank you all for not warning me about male children.

There was always some type of singing, cartoon on the television, and/or conversations between us. When I got off work, I think my husband and daughter use to race to talk to me. I had to listen to two people at once. Has anybody else ever experienced that? You must become SuperMomWife! That name has a ring to it.

After May 2016, all of that changed. I went from having a house full of noise to complete silence. You could hear a pin drop if you were still enough. I don't watch a lot of TV, but I remember turning on the TV just to hear some noise in the house while I worked. I was alone. Eventually, I adjust to the silence…but I think I would prefer noise over silence.

During that time of loneliness, I depended on God so that I wouldn't get depressed. The saying "an idle mind is the devil's workplace," is true. Because that's when the enemy will try to tell you differently than what God has said.

Kick him out of your mind and focus on God. God is with you. You are never alone.

Scripture: Do not fear [anything], for I am with you; Do not be afraid, for I am your God. I will strengthen you, be assured I will help you; I will certainly take hold of you with My righteous right hand [a hand of justice, of power, of victory, of salvation]. Isaiah 41:10 AMP

Question: What makes you feel alone?

_____

_____

_____

_____

_____

_____

_____

_____

_____

_____

_____

_____

_____

_____

DAY 7

Betrayal

I grew up in church. I attended church every Thursday (Bible Class) and every Sunday. I attended the fifty revivals we had every year. I attended every hat, shoe, and building fund program. I paid my tithes. I played the piano and preached the Word. Yet, I felt betrayed.

Because I did all these things for God, I felt He betrayed me when He came for my family. Quick insert – I didn't do these things for God because that's what we're called to do when we're saved and living for Him. But that's how I saw it at the moment.

How can this happen to me when I was/am faithful to God? Why would He do this… to me? Why did He do it to Job? Job 1:1 AMP states, "There was a man in the land of Uz whose name was Job; and that man was blameless and upright, and one who feared God [with reverence] and abstained from and turned away from evil [because he honored God]." Okay, God, you did things like this back then! You don't have to do them now!

God knew that day would come when He formed me in my mother's womb because He knew the plans He had for my life. Although I felt betrayed at once, it was all part of His plan for the greater calling in my l life.

Scripture: teaching them to observe everything that I have commanded you; and lo, I am with you always [remaining with you perpetually—regardless of circumstance, and on every occasion], even to the end of the age." Matthew 28:20 AMP

Question: Do you feel betrayed? Why?

_____

_____

_____

_____

_____

_____

_____

_____

_____

_____

_____

_____

_____

_____

_____

_____

DAY 8

Why did this happen to me?

As stated above, God knew May 2016 would happen in my life when I was in my mother's womb. Why did it happen? Some things we don't have an answer to and will never be able to figure out.

I put this in here to share insight. Most times we spend a lot of time worrying about things we cannot fix or change. Why did it happen? The most logical thing I can comprehend is God wanted it to. He's sovereign and He can do what He wants.

No, God is not punishing you! No, He's not trying to get revenge on you. He's not that type of God. I see it as this, whenever things happen in our life such as tragedy, God is trying to elevate us. When was the last time you prayed? When was the last time you fasted? When was the last time you studied the Word of God?

Because it's all part of His will/plan, we go through it and keep honoring Him. Has he not protected you and brought you out before? Has he not restored your joy and given you peace?

Focus on the promise…and not the process.

Scripture: Whatever God has promised gets stamped with the Yes of Jesus. In him, this is what we preach and pray, the great Amen, God's Yes and our Yes together, gloriously evident. God affirms us, making us a sure thing in Christ, putting his Yes within us. By his Spirit he has stamped us with his eternal pledge— a sure beginning of what he is destined to complete. 1 Corinthians 1:20-22 MSG

Question: What have you lost? How do you feel about it?

_____

_____

_____

_____

_____

_____

_____

_____

_____

_____

_____

_____

_____

_____

DAY 9

Grudges against God...

The pure, unadulterated truth! After the accident, I didn't go to church for about three weeks. If you know me, you know that's a long time to be away considering I'm there every time the lights come on.

When I did get back into the rotation, I was okay until a certain point in service. The preacher will ask us to praise the Lord for our family and I will sit there. I said I don't have a family, so I refuse to praise God.

From the time of the accident, I gave God praise because I didn't know what else to do. I couldn't pray but I could call on the name of Jesus! I remember telling the devil you tried to get me off course, but I still trust God. Little did I know, when I refused to give God praise, the enemy was slowly creeping in to build resentment in my heart against God.

This went on for maybe about a month or two. When I realized it, I immediately asked God to forgive me. I don't want to hate God. He is God and He is sovereign. If He kept me thus far, what makes me think He wouldn't keep keeping me? You know!

I repented and kept going. The enemy thought he would get me to turn against God for good but nope! Mission failed!

Scripture: Though He slay me, yet will I trust Him. Even so, I will defend my own ways before Him. He also shall be my salvation, For a hypocrite could not come before Him. Job 13:15-16 NKJV

Question: What grudges are you holding against God? Are you ready to be free?

_____

_____

_____

_____

_____

_____

_____

_____

_____

_____

_____

_____

_____

_____

_____

_____

_____

DAY 10

Trouble from people

This is the soap opera part of the book, but I must insert it because God instructed me to.

You would think that by me having to deal with my family no longer here, people that were close to you would act accordingly. Bro… Sis…. Ma… Pa…. the answer is no. I didn't think people could be so cruel to you when you're already down

I had to bury not one, but three people, and we were a blended family. My daughter was not by my husband so when all the families came together, it was a total of about six different families blended, with love. Some people talked crazy about me. They lied on me. Had things to say that were irrelevant. It was just so much. You would think they would spare my feelings but negative. These folks did not have a care in the world. As a grieving human being, I could have let it get the best of me, but I didn't. God kept me going.

If you've had to deal with this, DON'T GET DISCOURAGED!!! My Grandma use to tell me all the time that If I do right, God will handle the rest and I will have many stars in my crown!

I want to encourage you to do right and don't worry about the rest. I know... I know!!! Trust me, I know. But ignore all the family, friends, or anyone who's being negative, and focus on you and your healing. God will handle those that do you wrong! Stay faithful to Him and watch what He does on your behalf!

Scripture: For I consider that the sufferings of this present time are not worthy to be compared with the glory which shall be revealed in us. Romans 8:18 NKJV

Question: Did you see another side to family and friends?

_____

_____

_____

_____

_____

_____

_____

_____

_____

_____

_____

_____

_____

_____

_____

_____

DAY 11

Heartbroken

Losing loved ones, getting fired from a job, getting a divorce, all these things can contribute to a broken heart. In my case, it was my husband and two children. My heart hurt as if it never hurt before. It felt as if someone was piercing my heart with a knife. I was heartbroken.

I was reminded of the scripture, that says God is close to those who have a broken heart.

When our heart hurts, God is there to mend them and be our comforter. To be honest with you, I couldn't pray. I didn't have a pretty prayer. All I could say was, "Jesus!" I didn't have any other words to say. I was devastated. But the Holy Ghost was my Comforter and my Guide.

Scripture: The Lord is near to the heartbroken and He saves those who are crushed in spirit (contrite in heart, truly sorry for their sin). Psalms 34:18 AMP

Question: Have you felt heartbroken before?

_____

_____

_____

_____

_____

_____

_____

_____

_____

_____

_____

_____

_____

_____

_____

_____

_____

DAY 12

Am I being punished by God

Am I being punished? Every time something happens to us, we wonder if we are being punished by God!? No, God is not punishing it.

Whatever you went through was all part of God's plan. It may not be pretty, as a matter of fact, it was ugly, right? But God is there to comfort us through it all.

We don't know why things happen; we just know they happen. I like to think of it this way sometimes, maybe God was protecting them from something I could've never seen. I don't know what would have happened in their lives, but God does. God loves us.

Scripture: Beloved, let us love one another, for love is of God; and everyone who loves is born of God and knows God. 1 John 4:7 NKJV

Question: Do you feel like you're being punished by God? Why?

_____

_____

_____

_____

_____

_____

_____

_____

_____

_____

_____

_____

_____

_____

_____

_____

_____

DAY 13

Where is my peace?

Battle after battle. Struggle after struggle. When do I get a break? When will I see the end? When will I be happy again?

These are things we ask ourselves when we're going through. To be honest, it's hard to see the end of the tunnel when it's long and you're not almost to the end.

It seems as if when things are going well, something happens, and it gets worse. And to make it better, something else happens bad. It's like you put one foot forward and take two steps back. Does anyone understand me? Am I alone here?

Amazingly, God is peace. I'm getting teary-eyed as I write this one because I don't want you to give up. Giving up is not an option. You're so close to your breakthrough! Sis…Bro, it is right around the corner.

Keep the faith! Stay encouraged! Don't even wait until the trial is over, begin to shout right now!!!

Scripture: Peace I leave with you; My[perfect] peace I give to you; not as the world gives do I give to you. Do not let your heart be troubled, nor let it be afraid. [Let My perfect peace calm you in every circumstance and give you courage and strength for every challenge. John 14:27 AMP

Question: Are you ready for a breakthrough?

_____

_____

_____

_____

_____

_____

_____

_____

_____

_____

_____

_____

_____

_____

DAY 14

Will I ever be happy again?

I questioned will I ever be happy again because my husband was my friend. We met on Facebook. He said he knew me before then, but I don't remember. When I met my husband, I was tired of being in and out of relationships with men, giving them my all, and I never got a chance to meet their parents. That hurts! I want to be real because I want to help someone!

I've helped guys start businesses. Went on dates. Stepped outside the will of God (tell the truth and shame the devil) but still, nothing.

When I met my husband, I was skeptical. I didn't know how it would go but I knew I wasn't pouring out unless I was getting poured into. And that he did. He was my friend, lover, confidant and so much more. We thoroughly enjoyed our time together. We had our ups and downs, as all marriages do, but my husband was a great man, husband, and dad.

As of today, it's been six years. Often, I wonder, will I ever love again? Will God send me someone who loves me for me and is willing to put as much into the relationship as they are or want to get out?

My sister tells me all the time that my husband had me spoiled and she's seeing who will "top" him. Ha. We will see. I have asked God when is my next husband coming. I'm young. I know I'm a good woman and I desire to marry.

Scripture: I press toward the goal for the prize of the upward call of God in Christ Jesus. Philippians 3:14 NKJV

Question: Can you trust God during the process?

_____

_____

_____

_____

_____

_____

_____

_____

_____

_____

_____

_____

_____

_____

_____

_____

_____

_____

DAY 15

No one understands me!

During this time, I felt as if no one understood me. I felt as if I had no one so guess what, I only had God to depend on. My family was there but I knew they were hurting just as bad as I was, so I decided not to bother them. I wanted to be strong around them. I wasn't sad all the time but there were those times when I had my moment. The first few months were hard but after that, I was okay.

I would want to go places because I didn't want to be in a quiet house. I would admit, I had/have two friends that went with me everywhere. They were one call away.

During my time with them, I didn't want to talk about how I was feeling. I just wanted to enjoy their company and enjoy my time away from the house.

If you have someone close to you that you're able to talk to, talk to them. Don't hold it all in. It's too much to carry alone. I released to God. If you have someone, release it to them or God but don't hold it. Free yourself!

Scripture: You know my sitting down and my rising up; You understand my thought afar off. Psalm 139:2 NKJV

Question: Do you have someone you can talk to?

_____

_____

_____

_____

_____

_____

_____

_____

_____

_____

_____

_____

_____

_____

_____

_____

DAY 16

He's always there

There will be times when you want to give up! There will be times when you feel like no one understands what you're going through! There will be times when you want to say forget it and do what you want to do! Also, during these times, I believe God is building our character, molding, and shaping us into what He wants us to be.

Don't give up during these times. Guess what? The reason you hadn't given up, is that God has been strengthening you internally. Isn't it amazing how at one moment you think you're about to lose it and then within the next second, you feel strength or the courage to keep moving? That's God! Continue to trust Him as you go through this journey.

Scripture: Let your conversation be without covetousness, and be content with such things as ye have: for he hath said, I will never leave thee, nor forsake thee. So that we may boldly say, The Lord is my helper, and I will not fear What man shall do unto me. Hebrews 13:5-6 NKJV

Question: Will you trust and depend on God?

_____

_____

_____

_____

_____

_____

_____

_____

_____

_____

_____

_____

_____

_____

_____

_____

DAY 17

Why did He let me live?

I've thought about this over and over and the only thing I can come up with is that I have a purpose. Please don't misunderstand me here. I'm not saying my family didn't have a purpose. They left at God's appointed time.

The day of the accident, I was supposed to pick them up from school that day. What if I had picked them up? I wouldn't be here. I'd be buried beside my babies, but God had/has a plan for my life.

He graced me to go through that process of grief so while I'm here on Earth, I will help as many as I can get through it as well.

It's not a pretty process but it's necessary to go through to get to your healing. Let's heal together. I got you!

Scripture: For I know the plans and thoughts that I have for you,' says the Lord, 'plans for peace and well-being and not for disaster, to give you a future and a hope. Jeremiah 29:11 AMP

Question: What is God's plan for your life?

_____

_____

_____

_____

_____

_____

_____

_____

_____

_____

_____

_____

_____

_____

_____

_____

_____

DAY 18

What is my purpose in life?

At this given moment, I believe my purpose is to help others get through the process of grief.

I lost my husband and my two children. Often, I wondered if I would lose my mind. Would I have to take medication? Or would I have to be admitted to a mental hospital?

At one time I remember asking God, "am I grieving correctly!" Everyone thought that I wasn't okay because I was covered in the anointing. Then I begin to question myself and question God to make sure nothing was going to sneak up on me later.

God told me that I was fine and that I was grieving in the Holy Ghost. Because I've experienced this face-to-face, I can help someone else get through it. Everybody's situation is different, but I pray as I go farther that God will guide me on what to do, say and go to save the lives of others.

Scripture: I will cry to God Most High, Who accomplishes all things on my behalf [for He completes my purpose in His plan]. Psalm 57:2 AMP

Question: What do you feel is your purpose?

_____

_____

_____

_____

_____

_____

_____

_____

_____

_____

_____

_____

_____

_____

_____

_____

_____

_____

DAY 19

Doubts and Fears

My family is no longer with me. I was 31 years old at the time of their passing. Of course, years have passed since I've thought about this but sometimes, I wonder if I will get married again. If I was to marry, how would I feel about having children?

I had my daughter at the age of twenty-two. For the first four years of her life, it was just us and then I met my husband.

I'm young and I know I desire to be married. I know I'm a good woman and will be a great wife to my husband. If I have children, how will I feel? Will I tell them about their other brother and sister?

I told someone that if I do have another baby, I will definitely cry my eyes out because God entrusted me and allowed me to be someone's mom again.

If you're having these thoughts, don't think you're crazy. You are human. If you have lost your child/children and don't want to have more, that is perfectly fine. Don't let anyone make you feel bad about your decisions.

Scripture: Do not fear [anything], for I am with you; Do not be afraid, for I am your God. I will strengthen you, be assured I will help you; I will certainly take hold of you with My righteous right hand [a hand of justice, of power, of victory, of salvation]. Isaiah 41:10 AMP

Question: What are you afraid of?

_____

_____

_____

_____

_____

_____

_____

_____

_____

_____

_____

_____

_____

_____

_____

DAY 20

God is my strength

When you have no one or nothing else to lean on, you lean on God. God is my strength. There were times when I didn't want to call anyone. Had I called on them, there was probably nothing they could do but listen to my cry. But when I called on Jesus, I felt the strength I needed to keep moving forward.

No, I didn't have any pretty prayers. I was hoping the previous prayers were working on my behalf because there were some days when I couldn't think of the words to say. All I could say was, "GOD HELP ME!!!" With the utmost respect to my Father, that was all I had! When I said it, the Holy Ghost, which is our Comforter, comforted me and I felt better.

I cried. I screamed. I did all the above and I still called on God. Release it! Get it out! But ask God to help you get through it because He has greater strength than us all.

Scripture: The LORD is my strength and song, and he is become my salvation: He is my God, and I will prepare him a habitation; My father's God, and I will exalt him. Exodus 15:2 KJV

Question: What are you depending on God for?

_____

_____

_____

_____

_____

_____

_____

_____

_____

_____

_____

_____

_____

_____

_____

_____

DAY 21

Holidays & Birthdays

Yes, these times will be hard! I remember my first birthday and Christmas without my family. I was a mess. I didn't want to see anyone. I wanted to stay in bed all day and be isolated from everyone else but that wasn't God's plan.

After the first year, I decided to do things differently. During the holiday season, I spend time with my family. During their birthdays, I plan a date and I enjoy my time.

I refuse to keep putting myself back in a place of sadness. I choose to be happy, and I know that's what they will want as well. I can't sit around and dwell on the past while being sad. It's very unhealthy. I choose to live. What about you?

Scripture: I shall not die, but live, and declare the works of the Lord. Psalms 118:18 NKJV

Question: Do you choose to live?

_____

_____

_____

_____

_____

_____

_____

_____

_____

_____

_____

_____

_____

_____

_____

DAY 22

Will I marry again?

After our loved one has left, this can be challenging sometimes. If you're like me, a wife and mother, you're wondering will you ever get married again? Will someone love me? I was stuck here for a few months. After the accident, I decided I wanted to marry again. Not right after but some time down the road...before you try to judge me. So, my focus was on becoming someone's wife. Aha!

When God takes us through things, there is a purpose. Instead of wanting to be someone's wife, I should've been focused on why God was getting my attention and what did He want me to do! Whew! I know I'm wife material and I still desire to marry but at that time, my focus was on the wrong thing.

Once I realized this, I redirected my focus to God. Once I started walking in what I believe is my purpose, God started revealing things about my next husband.

So... here we are. I'm doing what God wants me to do but then I think about being married again. I don't want just any man, but the man God has for me. You know, my best friend, confidant, lover, and friend…all the above. Once I begin to align my purpose with His plan, He revealed the promise.

God told me not to worry! Trust the process because it will be worth the wait! I don't know about you but that was enough to keep me encouraged again and going.

To wrap this one up, it's okay if you desire to marry again. You are not going to hell for being human. Trust God and let Him lead you to your next relationship. Don't rush it. Do it God's way.

Scripture: I would have despaired had I not believed that I would see the goodness of the Lord In the land of the living. Wait for and confidently expect the Lord; Be strong and let your heart take courage; Yes, wait for and confidently expect the Lord. Psalm 27:13-14 AMP

Question: Are you ready for God to take you into your next relationship?

_____

_____

_____

_____

_____

_____

_____

_____

_____

_____

_____

_____

_____

_____

_____

DAY 23

Dreams

A lot of people say their loved ones visit them in their dreams a lot, but that's not my case. Every now and then I will have a dream but it's not a continuation of things.

My daughter has popped up in my dreams every time that I've had one about them. My husband and son, maybe once. These dreams were weird though. She was with me, and she was always around three or four years of age. At the time of the accident, she was seven years old. I didn't quite understand these dreams until I got someone who was a dream interpreter to explain. Once I spoke with them, it aligned with what was happening in my life.

God has a way of showing us things to get our attention. I've been dreaming since I was a child and most of my dreams come to life. So, when I have a dream, I don't take it lightly. Some of them and self-explanatory and some are not. When I don't understand, I need clarity on what it is. I don't want to miss the word that God is trying to get to me.

Scripture: And He said, Hear now My words: If there is a prophet among you, I the Lord will make Myself known to him in a vision And I will speak to him in a dream. Numbers 12:6 AMP

Question: Do you have dreams? What are you dreaming of?

_____

_____

_____

_____

_____

_____

_____

_____

_____

_____

_____

_____

_____

_____

_____

_____

DAY 24

You are Special to God

You are indeed special to God. Just because God allowed something to happen to you doesn't mean He does not care about you.

Of course, things happen to people all the time and I'm not being "judgmental" here, but I lost my entire family at once. Everything I had! That's tough! That's rough! I could have ended up in the psych ward, on drugs, in jail, in therapy...all the above! But God! Instead of looking at my family as something bad, I think I'm special that He chose me to go through it.

I wouldn't wish this on my worst enemy but when it's time for God's will to happen, it will happen. He knew that I would let Him lead me during this time. Some people are the opposite.

I know God has graced and equipped me to help others and that's what I plan to do. If He brought me through it without a scratch, I know He can do the same for you!

Scripture: Do not fear [anything], for I am with you; Do not be afraid, for I am your God. I will strengthen you, be assured I will help you; I will certainly take hold of you with My righteous right hand [a hand of justice, of power, of victory, of salvation]. Isaiah 41:10 AMP

Question: Do you feel God has left you alone? Why?

_____

_____

_____

_____

_____

_____

_____

_____

_____

_____

_____

_____

_____

_____

_____

_____

DAY 25

It's time to Heal

We've laid out every possible feeling or emotion and I may have missed some, but you know what you've experienced. Now we're to the fun part, healing!

Healing is essential for life. To have a joyous life, you must heal. Someone may say they don't want to live a happy life, but if that's you and your case, I can't argue with your decision. I would question and ask why not?

You were left for a purpose. If you've lost a child, you may have other children to live for. If you lost your sister, you may have other sisters to be here for and support. Your other family needs you. You need you.

I thought about leaving earth once. My family was gone so why was I still here? God reminded me that He left me here for a reason and purpose. I can't do anything but accept that, figure out what my assignment is, and walk into it.

How do I heal? Here are a few ways that helped me along the way.

Never stop talking about them. For some reason, this keeps me going. My children were young. I don't talk as if they once existed. Although they're no longer here, and I'm aware of that, I often reflect on memories and mention them every so often. No, it doesn't make me cry. It gives me the joy to know they lived an impactful life.

Remove all pictures and belongings. This may be hard for someone, but it's needed. My entire house was "our family things!" We were all in the house so everywhere I looked, I would see them somewhere whether through pictures, clothes, or whatever it was. I removed all pictures and belongings from the house. I still have the memories on my computer that I may look at occasionally, but I had to remove things from the house. I think it would have driven me crazy had I not. Does this mean I'm trying to forget them, absolutely not! It's part of God mending my broken heart so that I can breathe and not have a panic attack or cry my eyes out when I see them.

Celebrate life. As I stated before, God left you here for a reason. During their birthdays or our anniversary, instead of crying and being sad all day, I celebrate. Knowing they lived a happy life keeps me going! It's refreshing!

Scripture: Heal me, O Lord, and I will be healed; Save me and I will be saved, For You are my praise. Jeremiah 17:14 AMP

Question: Are you ready to heal?

_____

_____

_____

_____

_____

_____

_____

_____

_____

_____

_____

_____

_____

_____

_____

_____

_____

_____

DAY 26

No! You won't forget

Enjoy the moments because one day they will become memories. I have a plethora of pictures and videos in my phone. Most time we take life for granted and we don't take the time to enjoy life. I can assure you my family had a great time while here on earth and I captured as many of the moments as I could. Pictures, videos... I have it all and I'm grateful that I did.

When I look back on those pictures and videos, sometimes I cry and sometimes I smile. I can talk about them all day and night but when I look at the pictures, sometimes I get sad...and that's fine. Who knew that those moments would become memories?

I learned to thank God for my time with them. I thank God for choosing me to be his wife and their mom. I served a purpose in their life and I'm forever grateful for it.

Cherish the moments. Memories are forever.

Quote: "Cherish every moment with those you love at every stage of your journey." Jack Layton

Question: What are your favorite memories?

_____

_____

_____

_____

_____

_____

_____

_____

_____

_____

_____

_____

_____

_____

_____

_____

DAY 27

God has a plan

You were left here for a purpose. God has a plan for your life. I know right now it doesn't feel like it and you feel like your life could end and you will be fine, but that's not the plan God has for you!

As stated above, I was supposed to pick my children up from school that day, but God had other plans. Yes, I questioned it and wondered why He saved me, but He has a plan for my life. One of them is being fulfilled right now because you are reading this book.

But listen, pray, and ask God what does He want you to do? He trusted you with trouble, so He has a greater calling for your life. Consult Him and see what He says. You may be surprised, well not so surprised, at the results.

Enjoy this journey, unapologetically!

Scripture: And we know [with great confidence] that God [who is deeply concerned about us] causes all things to work together [as a plan] for good for those who love God, to those who are called according to His plan and purpose. Romans 8:28 AMP

Question: What do you feel is God's plan for you?

_____

_____

_____

_____

_____

_____

_____

_____

_____

_____

_____

_____

_____

_____

_____

DAY 28

Familiar Places

Visiting a familiar place after a loved one has passed is hard. I remember when I went back to church, I felt overwhelmed. This is the same church where we worshipped every Sunday, as a family. Now, I had to go in and leave alone. It was heartbreaking at first, but I adjusted. When I returned, I remember asking God to help me through that Sunday so that I wouldn't break down and cry!

Going back to work was hard as well. At my desk, I had pictures of them everywhere. So, to return and see the pictures, made my heart melt.

While at my moms' house, I was isolated in a sense. I didn't have to interact with those familiar places that reminded me of them. When I went back into these environments, I prayed so hard because it was hard. I needed the strength of the Holy Ghost to carry me and that's what He did.

Scripture: teaching them to observe everything that I have commanded you; and lo, I am with you always [remaining with you perpetually—regardless of circumstance, and on every occasion], even to the end of the age. Matthew 28:20 AMP

Question: Are you able to return to familiar territory?

_____

_____

_____

_____

_____

_____

_____

_____

_____

_____

_____

_____

_____

_____

_____

_____

DAY 29

Release! Give it to God.

One of my favorite scriptures is Numbers 23:19 and which says, "God is not a man, that He should lie, Nor a son of man, that He should repent. Has He said, and will He not do? Or has He spoken, and will He not make it good?"

One of the best things we have as a guarantee is that God is faithful. No matter what we go through, He will always keep His word and His promise. The Bible says He can't lie. That's why you should release everything back to Him. Release all the hurt, pain, and betrayal. Give it to God. He can handle it way better than we can. It's too much for you to carry. You must focus on living.

My prayer is that you live life more abundantly. Don't worry about what people say. Focus on God and He will lead and guide you in the right direction.

Scripture: Therefore, humble yourselves under the mighty hand of God, that He may exalt you in due time, casting all your care upon Him, for He cares for you. 1 Peter 5:6-7 NKJV

Question: What are you willing to release to God?

_____

_____

_____

_____

_____

_____

_____

_____

_____

_____

_____

_____

_____

_____

_____

_____

DAY 30

Permission to live!

I think you are ready to heal! I know this has been the biggest challenge in your life, but GOD IS FAITHFUL! Don't give up on yourself. There is greatness in you that the world is ready to see. Go after everything your heart desires and more.

I give you permission to be free!

I give you permission to smile!

I give you permission to love again!

I give you permission to heal!

I give you permission to ignore the haters!

I give you permission to travel!

I GIVE YOU PERMISSION TO LIVE!!!!

Prayer

God… thank you for my brother or sister that have just read this book. I pray that you will strengthen them as they embark on their healing journey. We know it's not easy but with you, it's possible.

Let them know that you are by their side and will comfort them in their time of need. I pray that the Holy Ghost will remind them of your word when they're feeling lonely and depressed. God be a company keeper and a mind regulator.

We rebuke depression and suicidal thoughts! Your sons and daughters will live and declare your works!

In Jesus' name, it is so!

-About the Author-

When you feel your only hope is dying, but God comes and speaks a word and tells you to, "LIVE," you hold to those words for life!

My name is Arletha Orr. I know firsthand what it feels like to mentally die and be resurrected with Christ. A traumatic event happened in my life, and I know God is operating through me to help others. I'm just a lady from the country in the state of Mississippi who enjoys worshipping God, traveling, and serving others.

I'm an author who will take you on a journey of how God brought me through the toughest times in my life to victory. I'm a minister and certified life coach. My goal in life is to help others, live a life pleasing unto God, and help save souls for His Kingdom. It's not about me, but it's about rescuing people for God's Kingdom!

Other Titles by Author

Thank You!

We would love to hear from you! Send comments and suggestions to hello@arlethaorr.com.

Stay Connected!

f Arletha Orr

f thegriefcoachms

⊙ thegriefcoachms

www.iShallLive.com
www.iStillLoveMe.com